At Capacity
A Short Collection of Prose and Poems

JAMIE M. GAUSE

TABLE OF CONTENTS

FOREWORD

To my mother,

I want to take a moment to express my deepest gratitude and love for you. You've been my best friend, confidant, support, and solace throughout my life. You had to grow up before your time to raise me and I am incredibly thankful for the sacrifices you made. You are the greatest gift that God has placed in my life, and your selflessness has not gone unnoticed. I've witnessed times where you were at capacity and yet you continued to go above and beyond for those around you. No matter who they were or what they had done, you were always there. I want you to remember that it's okay to allow others to pour into you, just as you have poured into so many lives. When you find yourself at capacity, please know that I will always be there to pour into your cup, allowing it to overflow with abundance and joy. It's not just reciprocation, but because you truly deserve it. I love you more than you know. Thank you for being a constant love in my life. You always taught me to go and be great, now it's your turn! I'm so proud of you for writing your first book, the world will truly benefit from your insight so they can go and be great as well!

With love,

Beautiful (Deja)Gause

At Capacity

A Short Collection of Prose and Poems

JAMIE M. GAUSE

x

At Capacity....

There I was standing at the elevator watching the numbers increase as it went up. I watched people standing next to me frustrated at the amount of time they had to spend waiting for it to be their turn to enter the elevator so that they could hurry to their respective places. We are always in such a damn rush!

My floor had come and gone, and I stood there watching people enter and exit the elevator for approximately 20 minutes. As the door opened, I noticed a large crowd of people in the elevator. I became nervous and was hesitant to join them on their journey. I politely declined the ride. I thought to myself; how is it possible for all those people to fit safely in that elevator. I started to survey the area to see if I could find the capacity limits for the elevator because in my mind; the elevator was bound to fail, give out, and come crashing down if people did not recognize, understand, and respect its capacity.

In that moment, I had to decide because standing there, watching others was not going to get me to my destination. It seemed impossible to decide due to thoughts popping in my mind, like stovetop popcorn. Again, my thoughts consumed me, what if I get stuck on the elevator, trapped for hours?

What if the elevator comes crashing down because of the enormous amount of weight that was contained in the tiny space? I am claustrophobic, what if I cannot breathe? I needed to move; one way or another. I was wasting precious time and confusing others by my unintentional actions. I pressed the button once more, the doors slowly opened before me. I took a quick glance and deemed it to be "at capacity,". Critically thinking about my current situation, I chose to take the stairs.

Reflecting on what I just witnessed, I realized, like that elevator, that I had reached my capacity in my life, in all areas and I had to decide whether I was going to take the stairs or allow myself and others to keep adding more to me until I ultimately broke down, destroying myself and others in my vicinity.

Knowing that I was going to someday explain what that meant for me, I searched the internet to help define what "at capacity" means. Here is the definition:

"At Capacity- At capacity is a phrase that can have different meanings depending on the context. It can mean **working at one's full potential** *and not being able to take on more work or responsibilities. It can also mean the current placement of utilities in an area is such that no more can be added without affecting the*

2

infrastructure. It can also mean the ability or capability of something to do, produce, or hold something. For example, "a room's capacity is the number of people it can hold, a factory's capacity is the amount of output it can produce, and a battery's capacity is the amount of electrical charge it can store."

I had come to the realization that after multiple failed jobs, marriages, parenting mistakes, lost friendships, and a life full of trials, I was at capacity; emotionally, mentally, spiritually, and physically. Being completely honest with myself, instead of hiding behind my smile, I accepted that I had been giving everything my full potential and energy, even things and people who did not deserve it. I was no longer able to take on anymore. I was DONE! That is when I had my life-changing light- bulb moment. If elevators have weight restrictions, if conference rooms, and stadiums can have occupancy guidelines, then there must be some boundaries for myself, my life. I needed to recognize this because others won't. People don't see your capacity; they just keep demanding more because they have something that they want or need from you. They often see self and you become invisible.

My proverbial elevator in this life has multiple floors and at each one, I was "at capacity" and needed to determine my next steps. I share this with you, in hopes that you will recognize when you are at capacity and that it inspires you; to take the stairs, when you need to.

1st Floor- In Love with Potential- NO capacity

If you are anything like me, you have fallen in love with potential. Perhaps, you were interested in a home that required a lot of work and appeared to be dilapidated. The home was being sold "as is" and you thought to yourself, "oh it has so much potential. Maybe you fell in love with someone based on the superficial good that you saw in them or the things that you thought they would become or hoped to become. Inherently, most people view these types of scenarios as non-threatening; however, if you do not have the capacity to take on this type of work or level of commitment then it can be overwhelming, stressful, and detrimental to your overall health and wellness.

Let me explain. Purchasing a fixer upper is a wonderful idea, if you have the resources and time that a project like this requires. It is truly an investment. Sometimes there are things that you cannot simply see or account for such as cracks in the foundation that are not easily identifiable; but are quite costly. Take my situation for example, when I purchased my home, it passed inspection; however less than 2 months in the home, the basement floor showed signs of damage, requiring a sump-pump, windows started to crack with replacement windows costing $680 a piece (I have 19 windows) and seemingly permanent fixtures seemed to decay like rotten meat. What a financial burden; fifty-thousand dollars? I was not ready financially or emotionally and the debt is still affecting me and my livelihood. Had I known about the deficiencies, I would have passed on the house (and my 2nd marriage). Like past experiences, I traded the known for all that I hoped for; and ignored the numerous warning signs.

My first marriage- I thought my then- boyfriend was a safe place. He grew up in the church. His father was a pastor. His parents are still together. He was smart, driven, and secure. I wanted the type of life that I thought he had and could one day provide for our family. In my youth, I thought, he had the potential to be a great husband and father. It had been modeled for him for his entire life. I came from a broken home, where my father had allegedly brought twenty-six other children into the world. I concluded that my husband had to be completely different from my own father. I could not have been more wrong; his representative showed up.

For the 11 years I was married, I don't think he was faithful for a single one. Being the faithful Christian that I was at that time; I knew he had the potential to change; every time he broke my heart with his lies and deception. I learned that having potential means nothing to someone who simply does not respect you, your body, your mind, or spirit. You would've thought that I learned my lesson after surviving a marriage that I let almost kill me. Nope, my hopeful, ridiculous self, did it again, and just recently. My second ex-husband: presented himself as someone who he simply was not, and I saw the signs early but stayed in the relationship; thinking he had the potential to change his actions and behaviors. It was not until I started to voice that I was "at capacity" that his attention seemed to be on me. It was too late because when he finally noticed me; my mind and heart had no capacity; no room, space, or desire.

<u>Not the Marrying Kind</u>

My love I've given away to the "not marrying kind",

Willingly, gently, forcefully, in hopes that change would occur in his warped mind.

Much to my dismay, despite me, he chose to stay… the " not marrying kind".

Material possessions, intimate sessions, my submission to his direction, forgiveness of his indiscretions, my pride, my confidence, My soul, I gave until there was absolutely nothing left.

The not marrying kind dines and swaddles you in the finest of things your heart desires not.
Cradles you in the bosom of pacification. Hypnotizes you with tender moments of nothingness preceded by passionate kisses and insertion,

Leaving you winded, gasping for air, and ultimately deserted.
Mentally he bashed my clouded brain against a concrete wall.
Bleeding, stumbling, staggering, he didn't let me fall.
My lover shoved me!

Rubbed my face in my despair.
Stepped on my back and pinned me there.
Freeing me from my hell only to fulfill his needs,
He spat in my face with each promise made to me.

He says," The day will come when you'll be my lovely bride....
LIES...

Because he is the "not marrying kind".

Forgiveness is...

Forgiveness is not a null and void transaction between us or a restoration of trust.

Forgiveness is freeing you from the gravity of the harm that you knowingly inflicted upon me.

Forgiveness is not an absence of me remembering how you took advantage of my vulnerability and love.

Forgiveness is freeing me from the devastating narrative that you choose to write and share about me.

Forgiveness is not subjecting myself to your presence and your power to crush my spirit once more.

Forgiveness is loving myself enough to let go of the disbelief and disappointment that I once had in you.

Forgiveness is not effortless or unintentional.

Forgiveness is necessary.

I forgive you.

Please forgive me.

2nd Floor- Bent not Broken

My entire life I was instructed to consider others more important than myself. I did as I was taught, and it has not gotten me anywhere aside from being slightly bent over and crippled by the weight of that whole notion. I put everyone and their happiness before my own; until recently. I no longer have the capacity to look people in their face and say "yes" when my heart, mind, and body are screaming "no," sometimes even, "hell no." I encounter this daily, with my job, my children, and my family. Repeatedly, I would neglect myself to ensure that other people were okay. Self -care were foreign words to me.

My mother taught me; that it is better to give than to receive and I believed this to be true; until I needed something or someone and was left empty, despite everything that I gave. Recently I was on TikTok, and someone said, Takers always recognize givers." I paused and reflected on my life, I was always surrounded by takers and then could not understand why I was always being taken advantage of. Your circle is critical to your survival.

On my job, as an HR professional, every day I am tasked with meeting people where they are and trying to help them solve their problems. As the world becomes more "sad," people become even sadder; depressed, anxious. Daily, sadness walks into my office, stairs me in the face, and says" what can you do to make me happy and whole. Although, my rational brain knows that I can't fix it, I cannot make them whole or happy; my heart and my prior teaching wants to make it better. I want to make everything and everyone better than what or how I find it.

In true Jamie fashion, I allow every person to transfer the weight of their life to my plate. To be frank, my plate is full, and it is spilling off the sides, making an unmanageable mess. I am at capacity, but my employer pays me to keep the door open and clean off my plate. The problem with this is that I cannot take on anymore; I have no one to whom I can safely transfer my weight to without being judged or dismissed. Unfortunately, due to the heaviness of all that I carry; I have been bent for years and if I continue to take on more; I will inevitably break.

It is not simply on the job challenges that push me to the edge of brokenness, but my kids as well. As a single mom-often my kids do not realize that I am fighting a battle every day to love, respect, and honor myself. Since the day I became a mom, at the age of 18, I have always tried to show-up for them, support them, and love them; meanwhile I failed to show up for me. Sadly enough, the people who were

12

supposed to show up for me or pour into me- often did not. By not showing up for myself, no matter how much I tried to be there for my kids; they were not getting the best version of me. I was constantly trying to pour into my children from an empty well. I still am to be completely transparent. When they cry; I cry. The worry, care, and concern for your children; never ends and it is exhausting and can feel like a thankless job. All that I give; it is never enough. Nevertheless, I have learned that I need to love them in their own space and allow them to sit in that space. Instead of trying to prevent them from feeling the hardships of life; I watch and wait. I stay close enough, so they feel my love and presence but maintain enough distance to allow them to figure out life for themselves and build some resilience.

My co-worker has a sign on her desk that says, "Everything is figurableoutable." It is a simple phrase but immensely powerful. People can figure things out, I must let them, and stop thinking that it is solely my responsibility. Setting boundaries for your life is necessary and only makes those angry who take advantage of you. I have learned that if I must make them angry to preserve my mental and physical health, so be it. I will no longer give access to people: employers, family, friends, children, lovers, and more who are not generally concerned with my values and well-being.

<u>Broken Crayon</u>

The dull, broken in half, sleeveless crayon- shoved carelessly to the side,

Imperfect and thus rejected in others' eyes.
Never tested or tried, the purpose of its form not even considered,
Melted for projects of curiosity or discarded as worthless liter.

Broken crayons to craft; the pallet looks amazingly anew.
Fulfilling its principal function; what it was created to do,
Composes masterpieces filled with imagery of color, beauty, and variance,
The broken form bears no noticeable relevance.

In a world of crayons without instructions, consumed with ignorance,
fear, and hate,
cowards will design a picture using a single shade, straight lines,
with no mistakes.

Don't conform to their absurd notions, don't accept their feigned
perception or fictitious portrait,
Experiment with any hue, ignore the lines, draw, design, or
freehand your own phenomenal sketch.

My beautiful child, never worry about your imperfections,
brokenness, missing sleeve, or dull point,
A true artist both understands and appreciates…… that broken
crayons still color.

3rd Floor- Suicide of the Sisterhood

While carrying the weight of the world on my shoulders, I noticed that a few of my counterparts look slumped over too. I am not naïve to think that I am the only one who has 1 foot planted on the ground and the other buckling beneath them. As a single Black mother, I watch others like me stand in a world that hates us, always at capacity. I knew the world did not like me, but for some reason, it felt more hidden before. Now it just feels real; real painful. Most recent experiences have shown me that they do not like me, walking my dog, buying groceries, in the media or in the boardroom. Some tolerate me; but will never accept me or like me.

What is even more painful is that at times, we (Black people) do not like ourselves or each other. I attribute this to the message of hate that the world spreads, similarly to COVID. It is not like the message of racism and hate is only taught to non-black audiences. It is preached to the entire world. We were taught to hate ourselves and anything or anyone that resembles blackness.

Because of this we often fail to show up for one another; in word and deed. For those of us who survive, by adaptation, resilience, and sheer determination, we do not share with our sisters; the lessons, actions, and opportunities

17

that help us to survive and thrive. This is not just for Black women, but I feel it applies to Black culture in a very generalized sense. Of course, this does not apply to everyone, but I have witnessed and been a victim of this toxic behavior. When a way up or a way out is discovered, why not share the steps you took to get there? Is it because no one simply handed you the guide or answer key? Fear of competition, fear of someone else succeeding?

Why do our "friends" stay silent in time of need? Where is the sisterhood that use to support one another? Making sure that each one of us lacked nothing? There was a time where we showed up for each other and each other's children. We watched our sister's children. We supported our friends by showing up to cheer on their children at games and events. If I did not know how to sew, my friend taught me. We shared recipes, laughter, sadness and made memories to last a lifetime.

What have friendships become? How do we form genuine long-lasting friendships? My mom used to tell me, if in life you have more than one loyal friend, you have more than your fair share and that you should be grateful. Mom was right!

I had to learn that being a friend; does not mean that someone is always there when you want them there. A friend

18

is always there when you NEED them to be and there is a difference. In addition, I was shown that a friend is a friend regardless of race. I have a beautiful life with sisters and brothers from every walk of life. Friends that I can rely on, confide in, and trust.

Life is hard, and no one is a mind reader. People will claim that you are not there for them when they never expressed a need for you to be there. I stopped expecting people, based on familial connection, race, or based on what I had given to others in the past, to show up for me if I never asked them to be there and that was liberating for me and the people in my life.

As I started to work on my mental health, I had to reflect on the people and friendships in my life. Tough decisions had to be made. I realized that some friendships had met their capacity. Although I appreciated them for the ride that we took together, it was time for me to get off the elevator and take the stairs towards relationships that elevate me to a place that I desire to be and not where they met me or think that I should be. It hurt too; but sometimes healing hurts. Forgiveness is a key component to healing the hurt.

<u>Forgotten Friend</u>

When I found me; inadvertently I lost you.

I do not miss the me that you knew.

I think that I miss you but suddenly; I am unsure.

<u>Too soon</u>

The ink is still wet, and the wells of my eyes will not dry.
My breath has not returned, and my chest still feels caved,
Years have passed but it still hurts the same.

The expectation of you exists in absolutely everything.
The scent of your presence still gently caresses the hairs of my nose,

…My mind is inconsistently damaged; it comes, and it goes.

<u>Wait for it</u>

I know you want to love again,
but just give it time,
Listen empathetically to whispers of your heart,
their rhythm, and their rhyme.
Move past the beat or repetition hook,
Learn and listen to the silence of love,
Dance to the beauty in your hopes and dreams,
Be swayed by the beat of your own drums.
Hear the sweet tap of love on the window of your heart,
Only let love in
when you are ready to emerge from the dark.
Close your eyes
Let anticipation and expectation guide your feet,
For it is then…
when you'll enjoy a love so joyous and sweet.

4th Floor- Keep the Weight Off

Complacency and inconsistency are the biggest contributors to a lack of progression, as I see it. Weight, as I mature, continues to be an issue. Most people think in medical terms when I complain about my weight. Do not get me wrong, I am a little fluffier and fuller than I would like to be right now, but pounds and waistline are not the only weight that I am referring to. Yes, I want to lose pounds, I am 4"10 inches and over 150 lbs.; my partner still thinks I am cute, though. Nevertheless, I am talking about mental and emotional weight, I found myself being complacent and hopeless as I went through my life; settling, thinking that this was it for me. Daily, I struggled with feeling like I had no purpose beyond being a mother. I spent months, contemplating; how do I make me better, my life more meaningful; more fulfilling? I felt stuck and trickery made me believe that I had no choices. I may not have always liked my options, but I still had a choice.

My first choice was to accept responsibility for being in the way of my own healing and happiness. As I reflected on my first failed marriage, I accepted that I never really deal with things; pain, loss, disappointment; I just bury them and hope that nothing agitates the burial site. I would bury it and then move on to the next thing and the next thing; my family can attest to this. I would remove or bury one weight and immediately put something else on. Not necessarily because I wanted to carry more weight but because, this is habit and because I was trying desperately to help someone else carry their own weight.

I am learning to keep the weight off and not like a fast-failed diet plan. I mean a consistent healthy lifestyle change where I look in the mirror and comfortably say that I like the weight that I carry. I had to become uncomfortable with carrying that weight on my back, shoulders, hips, heart, and mind. It became too painful; my body was near capacity. When the doctor told me to listen to my body; I did not respect it then. I respect it now; I respect and love myself which allows me to make choices that protect, heal, and strengthen me.

Fat People Problems

She looks so carefree, weightless, beautiful, and loved.
While I gobble guilt, shame, and trauma in high quantities,
Never satiated or full- I am a glutton for heartache.
Nothing fits, it squeezes the life out of me,
Unfastening the top button; It never helps.

As I expand, I stop caring about a cover up-
All my pain just hangs out.
Junk foods, stress, and worry, provide no nutritional value.
Pain is addictive like sugar; I am diabetic.

I feast in secret, the wrappers I hide under pillowcases.
The same ones I water every night with my tears.
This consumption of sadness is causing a blockage to my heart.
Destroying my ability to use my 5 senses:

I can no longer see beauty in the world.
Deaf to laughter that lightens and lifts.
Life tastes and smells like defeat and hopelessness:
Bitter and disgusting

Don't touch me; I am fat and unworthy of affection.
I am heavy! Filled with fat girl problems.
Lose the weight, lose the pain.

25

5th Floor- Closet Crying

My closet, most often, resembles the way my life feels or how my brain works, like a bomb just exploded and everything is scattered about. (Envision Monica's closet from friends, on steroids) I often close the doors to the closet to ensure that no one has visibility to the mess and disorganization, as it spills out of the closet and invades the entire room. This is how I lived my life, behind a door or closet, which was my smile, and no one could see the devastation that was behind the door. I spent so many years crying in my closet; that it started to feel like a prison, but it was oddly enough my only escape.

When I learned that my first husband had been relentlessly unfaithful during the pregnancy of my son and refused to end the relationship, I cried in my closet. When my closest uncle passed away, my closet invited me to come and take up some space in there. When my middle child tried to commit suicide, I made my bed in my close. When I was a devout Christian, I even made it a prayer closet, where I cried out to God to heal a dying boyfriend from Glioblastoma Multiforme (GBM), friend who's 9 year old son died from sickle cell complications, to heal all the cancer patients at the Barrett Center, peace, strength, health, protection for my mother and family, my kids and whoever and whatever else was on my list until I passed out in the closet.

Nevertheless, in this season, I have learned that everything has a purpose and that I cannot remain in a disorganized closet. Organization and putting things in their proper place have value. My fiancé is trying to teach me that. Please don't think that I am only speaking of clothes and hangers. Everything having a proper place refers to people, opinions, actions, feelings, emotions; we simply must make them fit where they are supposed to go and if it is determined that it does not fit or belong, we must be intentional about letting them go. Let it go!!!

The other truth that I happened to stumble across is that there is freedom in coming out of the closet. When I decided to not hide behind my smile and emerge from the closet; I eventually found a sense of social belonging and connection amongst those who had shared experiences. Knowing and conversing with people who were closet criers like me, deepened my levels of awareness and empathy in a way that allowed me to accept people for exactly who they are and where they are when I meet them. It increased my capacity to genuinely love myself, others, and connect in more meaningful ways.

In the Arms of Grief

I waited for you: my heart stopped.
Believing in your arrival: I aged to the point of death.
In silence I surrendered: Peace was never won.
Peering into the distance: I convinced myself.
Your voice and your face appeared: my desperate imagination.
No words just seeping rage: bottled up with tears that weep.
The earth did not bury you; painful memories keep you alive.
Lives on heartbreak

Unpacked

Hurriedly I put my emotional pen to my trusted notebook,
Our Noah and Ally love crippled me as a haunting flashback.
One fatal keystroke and upon us, I was forced to look,
And all the pain and beautiful memories, I slowly began to unpack.
Until I realized that I have nowhere to put
All the love that I still have for you.

Love of the Landings

Taking the stairs is not easy for someone who is out of shape and not conditioned for such a task. What happens when you take the stairs? Do you become short winded the further you go? Do you take intermittent breaks to rest your legs? You cannot or should not run up the stairs, which means that you need to be patient and careful.

Taking the stairs means that you cannot be in a hurry and that you must pace yourself. I will admit that I am not a very patient person. I want what I want when I want it and that settles it. Although, I did not take the elevator, taking the stairs was or is not automatically an easier path; it was just less crowded with less voices, noise, opinions, interruptions and allowed me to be authentically me without pressure, assimilating, or conforming.

There I was bent over, panting with profound sweat dripping on my forehead, and unable to take another step. Ever felt like you cannot take one more step, one more set-back, one more heartbreak, challenge, or loss? Felt like you do not know what you want, need, or where to start—well this is where we stop and rest in the landing area? The landing is where you get to pause and regroup. The boring uneventful landing is where you give yourself time and space

31

to be human and understand that you can take your time. If you are anything like me, a lack of movement means a lack of progress and I have learned that this simply is not true for everyone. The landing is not a waste of time. It is where you reclaim your time and sometimes your mind.

I wiped my brow, stretched my short legs, and caught my breath. I thought about where I wanted and needed to go—which was up, and focused my intention to the top. When you get this far on the journey it seems absurd to give up—although I was tired. Growing up, most children were scolded by their parents for using curse words. In my house, the word, "can't" was not permitted by my mother. It was not a part of my vocabulary- so when I was overwhelmed with the feeling of "can't" and wanting to throw in the cards on this unfair game of life; I knew a pause was needed to save my life.

I never had a plan to end my life, but before the pause; I did question often whether death would be easier—easier than all the things that kept me feeling defeated and without hope. The beauty in stairwells is that there is always a landing between floors, which means that you have consent to stop anytime you need to, without giving up completely; meaning that you never have to be defeated on your journey- give yourself some grace and believe that you will get there.

Reappearance

Quivering lips, watery eyes, and the face of failure
stared resentfully back at me.
The building bricks of loss and disbelief
Imprisoned and deprived me of my dreams.
Vacancy and do not enter warnings adorned my heart,
Hope's serial killer, mass murder,
my future mutilated and scattered in parts.
The limbs of my joy cast away
and thrown to the depths of the sea,
Concrete weights tied to my thoughts,
to ensure that I sink.

Deep sea diving, removed the weights, returned to the surface,
I successfully freed my thoughts,
Floating in the sunshine, against the waves and currents,
I persevered; I fought.
The shoreline illuminated
by the smiling clouds of survival and light of truth,
Staring in the mirror,
I witness the return of the joy of my youth.
Frolicking in the fields of laughter,
diving headfirst into imagination,
Fully future-focused on happiness and contentment
as my perfect destination.

6ᵗʰ Floor- Fractured Faith

For years, I identified with being a wife, a Christian, and mom. I served my husband and God with all my heart. I traveled the entire Tri-state with my kids for games, parent meetings, and more. I sang in two choirs, directed VBS, and could be found at the church anytime the doors would open. I was a servant to that life. I was nothing more; nothing less. My entire identity was wrapped up and swaddled in those titles. When I seemed to fail in all three roles of which I had poured my everything into, my faith was fractured. I had been praying since my youth to have a committed, healthy, and happy marriage which would result in a wonderful home to raise my kids in. I prayed and fasted for my marriage; I forgave everything. I went to marriage counseling. I did everything I could to save my marriage and when my best efforts did not work, I surrendered to God and asked God to heal my marriage. I spent every year praying for the same thing- and I felt ignored. My tears and cries went unanswered; so, with the death of my marriage; my faith began to slowly die too. It felt like the words wife and Christian were synonymous and suddenly, I was neither. I was completely and utterly lost. Oddly enough (or not odd at all), in that season, I decided to submerge myself in the waters of Christian fellowship in hopes of direction and revival.

Sure enough, God sent it to me. God sent me a forever gift, The YAMs (Young Adult Ministry), Keith Erin, Jamil, Alisha and a few others and they supported me and helped me hold it together through that devastating period. With all that they gave me, I was still searching for the God that seemed to not remember my faithfulness as much I was constantly reminded to reflect on God's faithfulness.

I was furious with God, and I never really dealt with the hurt, that I blamed God for letting me feel. I just kept burying it and adding more on top; to not feel the pain. I divorced and it almost killed me; literally. It felt like someone was ripping the skin off my body piece by piece and as if someone had taken a pair of sheers and decided to take my heart and make jigsaw puzzle pieces out it and throw away a single piece; so that it could never be made whole again. Not even God, who they claimed was the ultimate healer but had not healed little ole me and all those cancer patients.

What was I to do? I was not a wife. I did not feel like a believer and my kids were drowning in pain, and the faith that got me through every other challenging time in my life; was not fractured, it appeared to be GONE! The pendulum did not return for quite a while. I experienced hardship after hardship: a great guy I dated, died from glioblastoma multiforme.; my uncle died, who was like my pops, I got sick and had a hysterectomy at 38, I lost a really close friend because I learned that she was responsible for her relative's death and had been living a secret life, I developed an unhealthy attachment to a man who could not love me properly, my child tried to commit suicide and I made a poop-ton of awful decisions that are still having an impact. Consequences do not have an expiration date and it seemed as if my pain was never going to end.

I FAILED

I figured it out. God did not fail me. I failed me; I was not functioning in the right capacity. I am not sure that I ever trusted God. I concluded that I did not need to. I had always been the one trying to fix everything and everyone. I did not realize that I had been functioning under a different title, "Savior." When I could not fix it or save it, I just believed it was not meant to be fixed and I had no choice but to accept it. Today, I am so grateful to know that I cannot fix everything and that is not my responsibility. I am no one's savior. What a weight that has been lifted?

I also learned that just like you and me, God has a choice, and can choose what is wanted or best at any time. As I became more self-aware, culturally aware, mature, and experienced, I realized that God could have chosen something else for my life. God allowed this, which left my faith fractured—not GONE or forgotten.

<u>Every Day</u>

Yesterday, we escaped death, but we almost died,
Had it worked; your plan, I would have buried you and I
would have been buried alive.

Beating on the walls of an empty soul, my heart would have gone
to the grave, but instead every day, I am enslaved.
A slave to uncertainty and sadness; knowing that your pain is still
ever present with you.

And that every minute your mind denies you the truth- You are
LOVED and NEEDED

<u>Dear Mother</u>

Dear Mother, I am just unexplainably sad.

I am not ungrateful, and intelligence tells me that
my life is not all that bad.

The pain swallows me and regurgitates the same sad version of me.

My mind is enslaved and ultimately seeks to be set free.

Your super-mom powers and unconditional love are insufficient
for this war

My mind is confused and tired, I am afraid that I am unable to
fight this anymore.

RECOVERY ROOM

Oh God, I'm bleeding out, your voice is faint
And I can no longer see you.
I am laid out before you in need of a right-now healing

The trials I have faced have left me wounded.
With holes that no man can mend.
I need a revival and unfortunate end.

Oh God, revive me again and restore the joy of my youth
Apply your grace and mercy as a miraculous salve.

My heart heals in your hands as you breathe
Love, Acceptance, and Favor

You, Oh God, are the only hope that I will
Ever fully recover

7th Floor- This Time is Different

How many times have you left a situation, thinking that the next one will be different, but you take the same bag with you? In the bag, you carry around a ton of unlearned lessons, and you expect a different outcome. I am notorious for this type of insane foolishness. I have walked off jobs and out of every relationship with the damaging bags ready for something new. Just now in my mid 40's, I am realizing that nothing new was going to come out of that same old, tired, ass bag that I had been carrying around.

Prior to now, I always blamed the people around me for things falling apart (I blamed me about 10% of the time). My ex-husbands for being frauds. My children and boyfriend for being selfish, my mom for being controlling, my father for being absent, my employer for taking advantage, and now myself for being ignorant to think that I could not be part of the problem. I learned that I could not be the problem in its entirety, but I had to learn that I am partially responsible for the chaos in my life. I had to admit and heal.

So ...this time it is different. For example, when I was dissatisfied with a job, I used to interview and accept the first offer with money being a key motivator. Now I have learned to sit, watch, and wait (sit in the landing) for the perfect opportunity because there is not a job on this earth that I will sit and cry at my desk for, ever again. My mental health matters. I matter. I cannot say that after a failed relationship; that I will not immediately jump into another one (I am who I am), but I will say that I am now jumping with an awareness of hard the fall can be, and that I will recover. This time I am jumping in self-aware, honest, and unafraid.

This time is different because I am wiser about my capacity. This time is different because I am not in love with potential. I am accepting me, him, them, and God for exactly who they are and where they are; and evaluating whether their energy is what is best for me. This time is different because I have learned to be more flexible with myself and others, giving grace which allows me to bend and not break.

This time is different because I have learned to love me, which allows me to love the sister and brotherhoods to which I belong and to focus on the friends and family who love, support, and pour into me. This time is different because I am keeping the weight off, I have learned my limits and strength, and understand that it is not my responsibility to carry the weight of others and be okay with offering up my love and encouragement.

This time is different because I no longer live in my closet. I learned to go into my closet, retire the superhero cape, take off my HR hat, and come out with authenticity and courage, I can cry in the closet while organizing the heck out of every piece, putting in its proper place, as long as I come out before it starts to overwhelm me. I go to the closet for the sole purpose of selecting the perfect attire for the perfect day that I was able to see, knowing that someone did not get the same opportunity.

This time is different because even with my faith being fractured; I still find immense joy in the Creator and immense gratitude for the wonderful memories and experiences I have up to this point and for the years to come. Instead of trying to fix things that I did not break and that I cannot fix, I am selective about what and who I choose to give my energy and efforts to.

This time is different because I know my capacity. When I feel like I am at my threshold and unable to take on anymore, nothing more can be added to me without negatively impacting my infrastructure or that I can no longer produce and show up for my own life, I know how to decline the ride and take the stairs to a level that benefits me and those that need me to survive.

This time I am moving with intention, purpose, and in self-love which will empower me to keep moving to the next floor; no matter what is next.

Boxed Chocolates

Rise up beautiful, study and know yourself, and then decide,
To use each day wisely or to fearfully procrastinate and let it slip by
Your eyes; big, brown, and soft; keep them wide open,
Your heart in similar fashion until God has finally spoken.

Life is erratic, forging waves of euphoria and devastation.
Decisions must be made but with an adequate amount of hesitation.
Waves whip the core of your soul,
Shaping your character and your person.
The outcome of life's mysteries, you can never be certain.

Love or leave, try or not, stay or go, succeed, or fail, win, or
lose. Sometimes by choice, others you won't get to choose.
Live the best possible life my love, even when it hurts,
Always find a way to believe in yourself and trust in your
God-given worth.

My love will not fail or falter, no matter the victories or trials you
go through. So, when life gets hard; kick, scream, cry, do whatever
you must do. Remember to be true, brave, and strong, and just
DO NOT QUIT

Cause life is like boxed chocolates;
You never know what you will get.

<u>To the Greatest</u>

There is no perfection in family dynamics, but I would
choose mine, every single time.

From the maternal alpha to the newest seedling,
my loving village is a gift divine.

The woman who carried me in her womb continues to
carry me in her loving arms.

The children I birthed and the offspring from
my brother's union; they color my life with laughter and love.

My uncles and aunts sing melodic songs of joy and sweet
memories that I hold so dear.

My siblings' (in-laws too) reassurance that no matter how
far away they are; they are always near.

The unexpected gift of a bonus father who stepped in and
stepped up to play his part.

To those who I failed to mention, I love you- charge it to
my head and not to my heart.

8th Floor- Now, GONBGR8!!!

Holding tightly to the rails in the stairwells, using the landing and by placing one step in front of the other, I finally reached my destination- my final stop (for now). Along the way, I could have used any exit or hopped on a crowded elevator, but I took my time and stayed the course, and I am better for it. They say that the race is not given to the swift or to the strong but to those who endure to the end. In less words, DO NOT GIVE UP. A message that never tires and never loses its power. As long as we live; we will endure things that make us feel like it is a hopeless situation and like giving up is the only option. Do not consider giving up as an option at all. Remove the word, "can't" from your vocabulary just like my mom forbade the word in our household. You can do this!

When you are at the top, take a moment to take it in and remember how you got there, because you will need to recall your past victories, when you are faced with present and future challenging moments in life. In recalling, your perseverance through the trials of your life, it should encourage you as you start your next journey.

49

Our journeys will not be the same so deciding whether to take the stairs or to ride the elevator is solely your choice. That is the beauty in life; that you get to choose how you get there. Just promise yourself that you will get there no matter what weight life tries to throw on you.

When you function outside of your capacity; not only do you endanger yourself, but you potentially hurt others around you. Be vigilant and don't take on too much weight or weight that does not belong to you; this means intentionally respecting when you are at capacity; and taking action to minimize the loads that you are carrying and then keep moving forward.

GONBGR8, it is my license plate, but it is also my life's motto. I have always told my children that no matter what they do; be great at it. If you are going to be a janitor; be the best damn janitor there is. If you are going to practice medicine; be the best practitioner, you can possibly be. Living out my motto, has helped me to keep going on my journey; so, I share it with you in hopes that you will take this with you on your journey!

Go and be great (GONBGR8)!

Give thanks for absolutely everything- even the things that do not feel so good.
Own it- take responsibility, show up for yourself, use your voice, and continue to learn.
Never give up- appreciate the landings, pause on your journey, but do not quit.
Be authentic- be you; surround yourself with people who value (your circle), believe in, and support you.
Give Grace: You need it and so do others. Be kind to yourself and others. Forgive 1st!
Remember your why. Stay focused on why you are here and what you want/need to accomplish. Resilience: build it
8 – Eighth floor, 20th floor- regardless of how many floors you need to take to get there- believe in yourself; you will get there.

Proper Placement of the Crown

With forethought and meticulous calculation,
you were formed for greatness,
Enlightened and benevolent
witnesses prepare for your elevation.
Spectators and hateful hearts
prey on your victory with suppressive tactics,
Do not be fooled or distracted
by their hurtful and childish antics.

Head lowered only to await
the proper placement of your royal crown,
Rise up, stand tall, strong, firm
and of yourself; be proud.
Don't let cruel jokes, haughty laughter, doubt,
or difficulty freeze you dead in your tracks,
Do not retreat; let your love and success
be your defense and weapon of attack.

When wronged, take time to get mad,
cry, or scream to release the pain,
Don't let it consume you, let it go
you have so much to gain.
Possessor of extraordinary gifts,
charisma, and fortitude- expectations are high,
Be honest with yourself and others; don't be deceptive,
Remember nothing great comes from lies.

When life is unfair, and you feel that no one understands.
Look into the crowd,
I'll be chanting and screaming as your number 1 fan.
In life and in love...
remember; even when you are beaten down,
Hold your head up high
And readjust your crown.

53

Thank you to all who supported and loved me when I was not my best and at capacity.

ABOUT THE AUTHOR

Ever since I can remember, I have been on the move. Born prematurely, on an army base in Petersburg, VA, I started my life journey. Along the way, my family was stationed in Italy for a couple of years until we moved to Detroit Michigan, the place that I will forever call home.

My family relocated to Cincinnati, Ohio where I have spent most of my life. Graduated from Winton Woods High School, Xavier University, and the University of Phoenix. A mother of three children, 26,20, and 17, I spent my late teenage years and early twenties and thirties raising children, tirelessly serving, loving, and supporting my community, church, family and friends.

I have been an educator and HR practitioner since 2005 in various roles; teacher, Regional VP of HR, etc., consistently devoted to professional and personal development. I received my master's degree, started a doctoral degree program, owned a barbershop, am a member of the greatest sorority on earth, Delta Sigma Theta, and can carry a remarkable tune.

I have always had a love for language, whether it was singing words with a mic in my hand or putting my pin to paper. Every life I believe has a soundtrack, which tells a story of one's past and present. I wrote this book to tell my story and to encourage myself and others to live out loud, tell their story and sing their song because there is freedom is applauding yourself, being your own biggest fan, and taking center stage of your own life.

Jamie

Made in the USA
Columbia, SC
18 March 2025

55318255R00037